Two Menus

RACHEL DEWOSKIN

Two Menus

THE UNIVERSITY OF CHICAGO PRESS

Chicago and London

The University of Chicago Press, Chicago 60637
The University of Chicago Press, Ltd., London
© 2020 by Rachel DeWoskin
Published 2020
Printed in the United States of America

29 28 27 26 25 24 23 22 21 20   1 2 3 4 5

ISBN-13: 978-0-226-68217-4 (cloth)
ISBN-13: 978-0-226-68220-4 (e-book)
DOI: https://doi.org/10.7208/chicago/9780226682204.001.0001

Library of Congress Cataloging-in-Publication Data

Names: DeWoskin, Rachel, author.
Title: Two menus / Rachel DeWoskin.
Description: Chicago : University of Chicago Press, 2020. | Series:
    Phoenix poets
Identifiers: LCCN 2019024339 | ISBN 9780226682174 (cloth) |
    ISBN 9780226682204 (ebook)
Classification: LCC PS3604.E927 A6 2020 | DDC 811/.6—dc23
LC record available at https://lccn.loc.gov/2019024339

♾ This paper meets the requirements of ANSI/NISO Z39.48-1992
(Permanence of Paper).

For KIRUN KAPUR *and* FREDERICK SPEERS,
co-poets of my youth and life.
For our teachers forever,
ROBERT PINSKY, ROSANNA WARREN,
and DEREK WALCOTT.
And in fierce memory of
DESPINA CHRISTOPHI.

CONTENTS

ACKNOWLEDGMENTS

I am grateful to the following publications, where some of these poems first appeared:

Academy of American Poets' *Helen Burns Poetry Anthology*:
  "Love Poem from South China"
Agni: "Parting at Changgan" (translated from Li Bai's 长干行)
  and "Without"
Asian Jewish Life: "Chinese Highway"
Grolier Poetry Prize Annual: "Public Relations, Beijing"
Heartland Journal: "Wake Up" and "Chinese Highway"
Jam Tarts: "Extreme Sports"
Nerve: "Joint Venture"
New Delta Review: "The Caretaker's Daughter"
New Orleans Review: "American Highway"
Ploughshares: "Two Menus"
Seneca Review: "The Blind Massage Parlor" (as "The Blind Massage Parlor
  on Maizdianr Street") and "Love Poem from South China"

I am also grateful to Cui Jian for permission to use my translation of his song
"Power of the Powerless."

This collection and I benefited from so much solidarity and support that
my gratitude is difficult to overstate: to my poet cohort in Boston; to Rob-
ert Pinsky; Rosanna Warren; Derek Walcott; Kenneth Koch; Anne Carson;
Randy Petilos; Jill Grinberg; Chen Daming; Chen Shanying; Cui Jian; Ki-
run Kapur; Fred Speers; Vicky Henry; Christine Jones; Julia Hollinger; Lara
Phillips; Donna Eis; Cheryl Strayed; Emily Rapp; Rachel Cohen; Suzanne
Buffam; Jericho Brown; the M Literary Residency in Shanghai; the Mac-
Dowell Colony; my inimitable students and colleagues at the University of

Chicago; the best parents, readers, and people, Kenneth and Judith; my radically loving in-laws, Bill and Bernardine; my hybrid toddler/tween muses, Dalin and Lightie; and my first and final reader, co-everything, and hot star, Zayd Dohrn.

Two Menus

THE BLIND MASSAGE PARLOR

Doctors Han and Wang run the love
heart massage in one of Beijing's two
and a half billion broken alleys.

"You'll recognize it by the red
awning," Dr. Han says on the phone.
And when I do, I wonder who told him.

Later, on one immaculate bed in a row
of seven, I feel Dr. Han's fist wedge
between two innocent bones in my shoulder.

He accompanies the soundtrack of my
gasping with a simple statement:
"We hated *Titanic*."

I shift my weight on the straight, white
table. And arch my eyebrows, a
gesture Dr. Han overhears.

He rests his right hand for one
thoughtful moment on my spine
and explains. "The story was stupid

with its music. Your American
Hollywood knows what about love? Nothing
in that movie fit."

I make shy eye contact with the client
in a bed across the row. We are the only two
here today. I think she loves *Titanic*

from the delicate way she lifts
her neck to look at me, confused.
I smile and replace my face

into the massage table's dark
space. Maybe Dr. Wang and Dr. Han
also smile—at each other over us,

because Dr. Han says, "We've been
married for eighteen years. We feel
what other people just see."

Only after Dr. Wang, his wife
of eighteen years, giggles like a
movie star in love, does he turn

his attention and hands back to me.
"These days we have a lot of foreign clients!"
he remarks. "How do you say in English:
Does this hurt?"

THE CARETAKER'S DAUGHTER

I learned about sex on the swings at my grandfather's
farm. Pumped, watched the tongues of my polka-dot
Keds, dizzy spinning in Ozark sun dangerously close to
torching my toes every time I went high, ballerina pointing.

The caretaker's daughter, Faith Dickson, said
Well we did it the same summer she let me try her
taffeta dress. I danced on dry grass in fuchsia, sounding
like crispy leaves, imagining tan legs and ninth-grade

high heels. She wore coconut suntan lotion and a halter. Only
that morning, taking breakfast scraps to the pigs, I saw her
come out of the house and kiss Kinny goodbye. Barefoot
in the dirt, I fed last night's corncobs to ponies whose huge,

square teeth grazed my hand. Kinny's long hair framed his head,
didn't swing even though the kiss went forever. His face was
like a television set, but I said nothing, not even *Hi, Faith*, just
put my shoes back on when he drove down Glade Chapel Road.

We had sour cream and onion potato chips for breakfast, she said,
and I was quiet swinging but powerful on the playground
all fall knowing doing it means you can eat potato chips
and drink Coke for breakfast like Faith said I couldn't wait.

LOVE POEM FROM SOUTH CHINA

The tropical infection traced a map
up my finger, and standing outside
the Kunming Red Cross Hospital,
we watched this white rabbit eat

Christmas poinsettia before we found
the doctor named Wen. Registration
for the operation cost three kuai five,
equivalent to twenty-seven cents.

Dr. Wen pointed two fresh, ready
fingers at his table and repeated
(in English) *operation*. After the lecture
on pus and abscess, you expressed

nonchalance at the sight of his knife (he
unwrapped it, you said, optimistic), and I
whispered translations into the shirt
where I buried my face at your waist.

When Dr. Wen sliced the finger
like tropical fruit, the leather taste spread
to the back of my mouth. *Operation*
your belt Chinese vocab abscess

operation white rabbit red plant. The day
went on outside, and when I noticed it
again hours later, I had stopped
screaming. The bandages were just

gauzy hotel curtains, angels in fluttering
light. When I rolled from the shadows
of hospital shock, you introduced me to
my finger. Gored and masked criminal

bandit! Escaped from the Red Cross, you
said: Finger X. Read a passage from *Our
Man in Havana*. Yes, China, Havana, nary
a trauma; we double wrapped the digit's

disguise with a plastic shower cap and swam
off the coast of Hainan. But just to be safe,
you carried me through the water with my hand
raised like a torch above the waves.

NEIGHBORHOOD KIDS

That boy liked to play

    a game in which he took his

        pants off. I was
        a witch who caught him, stripped his

        underwear and there we were.

      I kept suggesting
checkers with our brothers, but no go.
      Evenings, we went swimming,
all the kids. Horseflies

    hovered heavy in the summer taking place above the pool, but
      I stayed under
    gelatinous water, moonlit, cold. Flies liked dusk thick,

      swam best in air so fat they stuck, swooping slow as amber, timing
        bites of our chlorinated arms and faces. We screamed

        with clean pain each time but laughed too,
        as kids will, coming up, breaking the surface
        of the water again and again getting bitten,

                        gasping in

TWO MENUS

Outside McDonald's downtown
in Beijing, I board a bus bound
for mountains with Xiao Dai,
who carries equipment, asks why
I have to be so headstrong.
I say nothing. We belong
to a climbing club. Sheer rocks.

        *

It is better to be the head of a chicken
than the tail of an ox. Men mention
wisdom whenever I disagree
with them. I am roped in, belayed. If we
fall, we all fall. My fingers are between
a thin ridge, sideways, gripping. I lean
down to tell Xiao Dai it's better to be
neither chicken nor ox. He can't hear me.
The rope swings, flicking sparks off cliffs.

        *

Translation is insurance. With just
enough to cover what we must,
we speak only where there's overlap, conserve
our syllables, expressions, every move.

9

*

The restaurant in Beijing called Bitterness
and Happiness has two menus: the first of excess,
second, scarcity. We order flesh
from one and from the other, grass.
The Chinese language has
77,000 characters Xiao Dai regards as
evidence. When I ask of what, he is putting
roots on my plate. *Love*, he says. My footing
gets rocky around these matters of fact.
A word for each affair? The waiter is back.

ARTICULATION

On the porch my father said his mother *wouldn't make it*. He sipped from a cup

as the screen door shuddered my little brother out in a metal gust.

We stood still and skinny, leaning on a railing

over which the night blew like a superhero cape. *Organs* and *failing*,

some other words I didn't catch. My brother wore Batman Underoos and a face

mask—we stared at each other, our grandmother's beautiful power erased,

so that when our father gagged, we imagined fear, sorrow, or both,

but he coughed out a moth

chasing it with a gulp of the drink

it had drowned in, knowing suddenly the weight

of a wingspan in his (next-up) throat.

CHINESE HIGHWAY

You wanted to take an overnight train from Xi'an,
        but I hired the driver named Yang, who danced as he drove. "Yan'an
song," he said, gesturing prettily with his right hand.
        You rolled your eyes and started up again—

We should've taken—but stopped talking
        just as he stopped singing
at the accident. Three trucks had collided
        and were nothing now but burning metal, ruined

in the road. We gaped, maybe relieved machines we make are
        not stronger than we are. They gushed radiator water—
sunlit oil made the drivers' graveyard holographic,
        their bodies so small in the tangle of traffic

trying to move. A farmer came to sell soda, trucks to claim remains, clear
        passages for cars. We moved through, fear
our vibrating quiet. Driver Yang looked in the rearview mirror
        at us, said, *One of those trucks was carrying bees*. We drove into a sheer

curtain of buzzing, giant smoke rising from honey-truck eleven,
        whole road steeped in sugar glass. We covered our stinging eyes even
as Yang went back to the song about love: *Treasure, if I don't see you for one day,*
        I cannot swallow a single strand of noodle. Please say you'll stay—

AMERICAN HIGHWAY

All that land blasted flat with dynamite blew by,
      cliffs gone, highway blank as white noise. On my
          back across the backseat, trees went upside down,
the branches bats and icicles, nooses. We moved fast across
      other people's roots: Detroit, Cleveland, the animals and silos,
          highway lines sucked underneath the stomach of our car.

Each house we passed I thought I could have ended
      up in easily. Reading *Lolita*, imagined my
          foot on the gas, speed inside me, thin limbs
in a backseat pretzel tangle. I was thirteen. Shell station,
      seeking out the gaze of a man pumping, daring him
          to be middle aged, sophisticated, drama for my drive.

But he pulled away without a sigh in my direction. Fire
      of that summer, Dave B., on his way to Oberlin, had taken off
          my shirt. Fresh memory: my best friend's basement, musty
on a coolish night I could taste the rest of my life
      in his mouth. Sam Adams beer, clove gum, the whole Midwest.
          Rough couch against my newly naked back, this feeling

also had a taste—a breaking off in chips and melting
      peanut brittle one I wanted, want. Dave B. is now
          Hasidic, now Lolita would be sixty, now I'm married
              with a baby, once you see you—see?—you're gone.

FOUR YEARS OF WINTER

Today, school again in the wrong
    boots, dress. Kari S. writes along
        my locker *bitch*. She still
            leaves me notes: *I hope you die*—I will

retreat to rhyme (Billy Joel, Sylvia Plath). Books,
    not the bright, hot words or hallway looks,
        falling by my stupid feet, see Kari's perfect
            new, black Reeboks. Algebra. Seventh subject,

        high-pitched whispers freeze my blood—
      like grape pop fizzing up my wrists and neck. Good
    thing they sit behind me, can't see
my face fill. My mother calls "just jealousy"

so many purple Trapper Keepers filled with notes to me:
    slut, goner after school, once, *cunt*. I agree
      that Kari takes the lead, the cake. Decades
        can sand rocks down, and soon this, too, fades

      into dirt. Eighth grade. Nancy K.
    shoots herself in the face. The papers say
      she was playing, say *accident*. Her parents say so too. But we
        knew her (something we'd made ourselves) misery.

PUBLIC RELATIONS, BEIJING

I.

When Jane fell in love with a Kuwaiti,
the embassy warned him against Chinese

girls. *We'll revoke your scholarship,*
they said. He was a student

who ignored the rules
for love (to hear Jane tell it)

and traveled with her that summer,
eating sunflower seeds. Unfamiliar

language rose and broke from their
throats. She calls him

Old Ma still, a leftover
nickname for Madallah.

II.

The sky in Beijing is blank
the day Jane starts to talk

about her love. *We said I was his
guide,* she laughs, because they were

caught in a hotel with no marriage
or money. In seven months

of self-criticism at school, she never
confessed that she loved him. *Anyway,*

she says, *he went home for American war,*
so no one cares about this love anymore.

III.

Every day of 1995 Jane writes a letter
to Lao Ma. He does not write her

because he's a diplomat and isn't
allowed to write to Chinese girls.

She and I work in an American
office advising on foreign

investment in China. Jane does not like
the translation our firm has given

General Motors. It means *mediocre*
motors in Chinese, she tells me. So we

write a report recommending revision.
But GM says it's too late to change

their name no matter what.

IV.

When I meet Madallah in 1997,
Jane has already loved

three other boys and warned me:
Lao Ma is not the same anymore.

Now, she says, *he is a successful
career and a failed personality.*

Per our personal free-trade language
arrangement, we leave each other's sentences

alone. *Madallah has married an
arranged woman* and come back

to Beijing to polish his Chinese
without her. We meet at Uncle Sam's

Fast Food. He and I have only Chinese
in common, so when I ask what

it's like to be married
to him, he cannot gauge my tone

and gives me the straight answer
I want: *In my country*

*women are like queens; no one
disrespects you on the streets.*

V.

Jane and I have an emergency
dinner at Three Four Man, our

favorite Japanese restaurant. Her eyes
are wide and tired. *Our dream of love*

is over, she confirms. Madallah's new
wife has to sit in the back of the house

with a cloth over her face when
men come to play cards

(five nights a week). I am surprised
he isn't busier with matters of the state.

Jane says: *When he told me this, I*
shouted. I think her life must be terrible.

But over dessert she asks me, do I
think his wife is pretty. *I know this*

is a terrible question, she says. And I
know what's coming: *But if she has to*

wear a cloth over her head anyway,
then why couldn't she have been Chinese?

EXTREME SPORTS

Here the beehive, alive with potential
to give us a jolt that'll sting or swell

us up, make me shriek. A cliff? Let's jump, a cord snaps
back, keeps us from the dirt another day. Perhaps

we just like to come as close as the river does
to some thin lines. Here, racing this northern length was

our recent screaming feat. Rocks may smash a raft, back, the last
fact: water toxic to us and fish. We flipped into rapids so fast

white foam fountains spun us under until we were propelled to a still pool.
Salmon hadn't floated up yet, bellies burning, because it was cool

in May. Later that same summer it got hotter, and they
cooked. For now, our oars gone, orange kayak likely miles away,

we climbed onto a Klamath rock, shocked, giddily alive. I said, *Look,
an eagle*. It swooped close as a puppet to us. You took

my hand, pale and shaking with something. You'd be
practical and save us. But you asked, *Want to marry me?*

HONEYMOON

Highway 96 runs north, its mile
        markers mark cliffs sheering to a river. While
            we chat, a circle of turkey vultures eat
                us in my mind, await

                our bodies, lust to beak fresh bones.
          Their faces blush with blood. Red stones
    could avalanche at any time. Our vows went well.
We'll love, respect, and listen to each other, tell

good stories, stay together
        until whatever
            end we come to does us part. This rental
                SUV's a vulture too. We circle, circle,

                lost until we park. Who cares where we are? A guest
          or two threw flowers, blew kisses. We flew west.
       You say: *Each year at least one car goes over*
                    this edge. They have to fish it from the river.

                I put my fingers in your mouth. Water moves through
            a million shattered rocks below us, two
        stone shelves hold trees that rest
between hot gusts. They jut an offer to us: build a nest.

We strip our clothes, stay lively through
        our first nights married, new and naked, who
            we'll be post-this, pre-vulture still a mystery.
                Maybe baby, not yet ours, will know. We'll see.

FOREIGNERS

There's a language for other
languages. Burning

my bedside table
is a red dictionary. Night-light,
guided, partial escape

from my fear of this
illiteracy I live in

a dark constant: wonder.

Is everything simple, or is
emptiness just another

misunderstanding? Beside me,
tea has steeped all day

uncovered. I sip slow, still it
soaks my mouth with cold, leaves

a faint taste I can't read.

SEAFOOD

In the neon Rainbow Seafood Club,
        we remember the future before

                us: visible, audible, edible. Now past is
        long out of our range. Dark, estranged, we

    watch cloudy cases lobsters peer back from
eyestalks, walk glass-to-glass wall,

        sideways, twisting through crowded
            water with one tense and motion, present.

HOUSEKEEPING

A frog lives under dirt
      with spiders chicken-sized and violent,
chicken-eating even, but they love

this game frog, fetch
      him water, keep him in a safe
dark corner. With their fangs,

protect him well until, well—what
      is it happens to a frog? Kenny Rogers sang it
country. There *is* someone for everyone, turns out.

Even in the country underground spiders
      hunt fast meaty prey in packs, return at night to eat
their babies (taste like chicken). But they never

eat the sweet frog. Maybe love's a prison: green
      frog sweeper, insect cleaner: ants, ticks, mites—
enormous spiders dislike the tickly bugs he eats.

Not movie-worthy love perhaps but
      something workable, domestic. Virgin
marriage, homespun web, no swimming,

buzzing, no flies land from blue onto your outstretched tongue, no
      lily pads for you, no leaping. Beloved frog, you
are the very definition of a pet
            —eat your grief quick; keep kept.

NIGHT SWIMMING

Literally. Smoke off black water, boat wrong—

—moving away from shore—why? primal imperative, song

through chattering bones: turn around! humans are so

stupid, with your new year's eves, with what you show

each other: courage, manta rays, in this case. thus you rush

oblivion? slick oil from the motor is a blush

on the sea's sarcastic surface. you?—are nothing, are

wet suits of rubber, dots, plankton confetti you throw far

out, you are not the light you use to light it, to

attract rays to the surface, not stars or wishes, not even adequate to what you

try to see—you are diminishing, lowering your body into dark

so cold and total it's inverted sky, no air, this lark

adventure, lark *experience*, lark *authentic*, call

out from across the metal cage you're holding, face down, choking snorkel all

the sea inside you. here one comes. do not molest the manta rays—

they're covered with a precious slippery surface, guide says

but forgets to ask them not to touch you—this one

rising, giant, what! its entire middle, absent? cartilage/fun/

tire/donut/terror, you go boneless ringing in each other—creature who prefers

your feet, cheek, wet suit, neck, and fingers to the plankton—lures

you deep into a pure void water moving through the hole

a body's core reveals, pulls over your head, control

is ended you are finished now this minute will never be over will always run under

the next and next, your fear so sheer it'll double forever as wonder.

SEX POEM

Everybody loves a list.
Some language hot across these rocks
and then again, one edge of a bunk on

a dirty river steamer. Why
write? So you won't forget
what to get at the grocery store or

you yourself the way you taste still gnawing
at the surface even now. Who will be
the one to bury you? One: breakfast, easy

mantou, *steamed bread*, soy milk from a vendor
called Tang (means *burn* to me). Two:
I'm a ravenous animal. Three: our only constant?

Asking. Four: this cliffside drive
finds us vivid and alive. Five:
the driver is singing that song about love.

If I don't see your face for one whole
day, Treasure, I cannot swallow
even a strand of noodle. Six: he swerves,

just misses chickens, goats, a lone duck. Sun
pours in, broiling us through plexiglass.
Seven: live hand on my thigh as you hum

along with the noodle song. We know
cars and buses sometimes plunge over this edge—
Eight: what does that feel like? Nine: the cliff

keeps inching closer, scary, daring. *Come on
over*, edge says. Ten: of course
we'll both reply eventually: *Yes, yes.*

GIRLS AT 1001 NIGHTS

We were small-talk and falafel
    when she shimmered from the kitchen gold all
        over, tables suddenly full
            of hungry people. A beautiful lull

            in conversation, now she pushed her right
        side into air so thick the room bulged tight.
    A man in yellow blew fruit hookah smoke
and bellowed, singing, took a toke,

cheered. Were her arms graceful? They flailed,
    I thought, escaping the straps of a scaled
        bra, below which was all skin, her skirt low.
        Along her stomach a hollow

            scar smiled out, smart, angry sneer.
        Glitter made the room's light appear
    and disappear—thrown off too fast to catch. Her
hips spun the public circle, were

the joy of every meal. She flared smiles, brushed
    up purple chairs, arrived here last, a little rushed.
        The music stopped, she faltered, looked outside.
            Window: zero, instant winter. I looked too, tried

            to see what she maybe saw. But cold air
        seared the glass where an odd shape near
    the building stood—a tree? I couldn't see
past our blurry faces, superimposed, her/me.

BELLIGERENCE

Some of the temple cops were plastic toys,
others it turned out slammed real sticks
on the ground when tourists made noise.

Even the reals didn't sweat or blink,
but then some ducks walked in a line of six
across the courtyard hall in sync,

right where the emperor housed all
his concubines. This riled the uniformed guys. A flock
so disobedient, their feathers slick, no call

enticed retreat. One guard shifted his weight,
allowed his eyes to flicker over mine, took stock
of the extent to which he might retaliate

against small birds. I imagined roasting ducks
in ovens after skinning and hanging them by
their necks, embarrassed, featherless. Who plucks

the endless meaty bodies we eat
wrapped in pancakes? A wild cry.
I felt the guard's eyes on my feet,

orange plastic covers over my shoes
required to walk the palace floor
looked webbed and birdish, my body sudden news

to me. My friend on a ramp between some stairs said: ·
The emperor was so fat ten lackeys or more
had to carry his ass around. Imagine him in your bed.

It's disgusting. She pointed to a period room, three
feathered pillows, canopy, a dressing table,
lacquered hair comb, cloisonné, told me, *See?*

The women had to wait in here for him. Across
from us, the guard was staring, a test we were able
to pass: he glared at me, the ducks, my friend. *Hey, boss,*

she said, *your ducks are lost.* Thus dared, he didn't stir,
but she walked closer, stared right at him,
added smiling, *Even cornered beasts will struggle, sir.*

Another guard showed up then, pulling a suitcase.
He caught and shoved the screaming ducks in, grim
battle quickly lost. My friend held her game face.

STRAIGHT UP

Spotlight strapped above the eyes
  head into blank space, tilt back until
    what hangs sharp from above is visible.
      Lean forward for what might rise.

      So said can be unsaid, turns out, done
    undone, recast. Cast about fast, flail alone.
  Our bodies move our minds, guide says *climb*, says *don't look down*,
says *fear makes girls slip off the edge*, hold on

which girls are there
  scaling such hostile rocks in the dark, where
    is this cliff? Maybe there's no way, no me/her,
      night, no stars slicing a sheet of sky. Remember:

      remembering is falling. Vow to look down quick
    in fact, take stock of what leads this way, that, up, back, stick
  this landing. I'm dying to climb out from each contradiction,
fix what can't be fixed, belay by way of impossible prediction—

So fine, fall. Get up, love a rope, a net,
  intent. Grab at whatever set
    of truths a fighting crowd of selves may make, all
      our holds along such a sheer, sleek wall.

JOINT VENTURE

Xiao Ke parks his Beijing jeep
      outside the restaurant window
whenever we have dinner. He wants

to watch it while he talks. *I call it*
      Clinton, he says, pointing. Parked
on the sidewalk, it gleams. *Because*

it's a Sino-US joint venture. We eat
      sea creatures, and he serves me, dangling
legs and sprouts with chopstick precision

I never rival, even later, after five years
      of this friendship. It's only after four
that I am able to ask whether

he cheats on his wife. It comes up
      in a conversation about Clinton.
It's great to be an American commoner,

says Xiao Ke. *But terrible for leaders.*
      Americans like to talk about rights. But
they can't even have mistresses.

When I ask what about China, he holds
      my gaze. *In China*, he says, *no one*
asks this kind of question.

So I ask again, *Do you have a mistress?*
       We're in the car, and he replies, *You*
mean the French girl? I say, *I guess I do,*

and he grabs me, kissing—it's a choked brand
       of abandon, this taste of his pulse and a beat
in my throat, the closest I come

to an answer before it's a question again. He takes
       his mouth back to say, *I can only drive Clinton*
at certain times. Even American jeeps

must abide the highway rules. My
       hands return to me, dragging lap and
leather seat before I slip out of his car.

I WAS DANCING WHEN I HEARD

Through the slender,
      lively grapevine
that you're happy.
      Getting married, at that.
To someone else.
      Getting married, at last.

I was dancing.
      When I heard you're
getting married,
      I was dancing. And reeling
just a bit on impact, just
      a little impact. Just a bit.

A little alliteration may be
      mistaken for love. It isn't.
I was dancing. A step
      mistaken for fashion
by fashion's girlfriends
      when I stumbled. When I heard

you're getting married.
      Other clubbers even reeled
in sync. To a step mistaken
      for intention. Or dancing. I
was dancing, and the disco ball
      had a thousand insect eyes.

Married, how lovely. I reapplied
      lipstick to my horrible smile.

YOUR WIFE

To iron in your nineteen-twenties place,
      I fold the board out from a kitchen wall
while you're at work. I like to lie on small,
      hard boards these days, like waiting in a space

left warm by your white shirts. I stay as still
      as dishes, clothes, the words we put away.
Just see the ox as whole, you love to say,
      not butchered parts. This makes me want to kill

you every time. The lock clicks with your key
      inside it, suddenly you're pouring down
the hallway, filling our rooms with the town
      warm on your coat, skin, neck. Please let me be

      more than a kitchen witch. Someone complete.
          Just reconstruct this ox from scraps of meat.

WAKE UP

Dark, our difficult wonder, understands
this city's list of questions and demands

that morning be brought on again. Our town's
awake, hot pavement mirrors the sun, brings rounds

of vendors calling up their offerings—
fried dough, *soy milk*, vowels float over awnings

into spaces where we make our days. Noons
pass while we play life until the ruins

of buildings, bridges, lights strung highway-side
short out, we rise. Stall covers roll up, wide,

reveal sprays of light, fruit, spice, our trade
language alive. Pork bikes ride by, meat splayed

across back fender racks, to luncheonettes
for fire, ginger, numbing pepper. Markets

give patterns: feathers flutter from the block,
stretched necks ready for flight and bones for stock.

RETICENCE SCHOOL

The seasons took turns politely—

lined up tightly

waiting for the next teller while

pronouns exchanged letters, she/he smile

leafy parenthetical (which/what are

we actually?). Nightly, each star

lit the way for boys oiling their shoes and singing

into the wind while girls stood on tiptoes, winging

the gist as if with butterfly nets. So we caught

ourselves instead of what notes taught.

Nothing set straight, let's just call it this: we'll love each

other, naming or not naming, make words that reach

for chance, for a hazier age,

reveal like winter and melt the page

MY GRANDFATHER'S WIVES

The two make good TV: first dark, the second ice cube
clear and blonde. My grandma Mary, lovely diva,
      was herself more than one wife to Irv. Her mind split
up and fluttered like a shuffled deck. She lit the house
on fire when he was late. Her dinners were as beautiful
      as blue St. Louis days, and so was she. All that
bright wedding china shattered in a fit
worthy of a Disney witch. Irv hid. Cool basement with my father,
      building televisions, calculators, connecting endless wires,
starting Heathkit projects I found later when he died. Electronics were his
weaving, waiting for a time when she was back, OK, re-sane. It came,
      that time, sometimes, and then it went.
He married Eleanor, her opposite, moved out, moved on.
So Mary flew to Florida, bought herself a giant diamond ring,
      then died and left the rock to me. I have it on, three karat
if you can believe it, just about the size of a stage three tumor, but
square and flat and round at once. In fact, it's nothing like flesh.
      Oh, family brass knuckle that can't be destroyed, you reflect
crazy light, threaten to slice any glass in our path.

CARDIAC BREAKFAST

After Beijing, there's just time—
      US days parade by, military in green.
Helicopters, chickens, and dictionaries seem
          English in lines I'm in between.

After Beijing, sweet disorder takes over.
      Here language unfolds in a stroke overnight.
February arrives, inevitable surprise—I discover
        myself upside down out inside underripe.

So let's eat America together. Take this icy time
      zone, watch the weather, get married, play pool.
Let's make a deal: seal culture-shocked kisses,
        speak English forever, sound cool?

After Beijing, I wake up—starfish points,
      parched with salt, tasting lime from the water
flown over. Anoint, set me free, teach my language
        to speak me: I'm home and this alphabet's mine.

PRISON QUESTIONS

To see your brother's mother in jail, we drove

    the same highway she had, 1981, 2001, slow wove

        a tangle of side streets while you told me

            rules. But the guards made me take my pants off at security

        anyway, because metal buttons because I had gotten

    the earrings keys rings coins but forgotten

my place. Was I proud? Sweatpants up to my

    neck, yet the detector tantrumed, next my

        shoes socks shirt the tall one asked about my

            bra, a wire? 1981. Your brother's mother came by

                way of what? Twenty years ago. Remind me what

        remorse and terror. My bra was wireless, but

        I shed it. The jacket they gave me wouldn't shut,

I clutched for buttons, tried to keep my face still, try

  even now for calm. Some more alarms, one shrill cry

    —a child in the line of women behind me. Nothing left to peel,

  they shrugged me past, stripped a grandma next. Banging steel

    gates, black lights revealed invisible marks we could feel

on our hands and there we were: cement walls, one small TV screen,

  two books, a poster: *Read*. Stuffed bear. A vending machine

    spit out shiny packages of popcorn. She arrived on the arm of a guard,

    her face so soft it was hard

    not to look away. I tried to stay

  both here and in those twenty years, to know what to think, ask, say about decades gone, the meaning, men shot,

many families in this maw forever devastated. This was not

an intersection I'd expected. She held her hand out, fragile, small

as bones wrapped up in parchment, holding all

we'd heard and wondered. We shook (hugging forbidden), and she recited for me

a poem she'd written at sixty, about you three.

Your childhoods gone, it asked what men you'd turned out

to be. I didn't know much about

it myself. She asked warm questions, trying to see her

son in your family and you now in mine. Over

that table how many lives passed, so far away,

some rippling out. When we got snacks, she was embarrassed I had to pay:

peanut M&M's, potato chips, a Coke, sad salad plastic

wrapped. I tried to ask back, but language was elastic,

stretching snapping never meaning what I wanted to mean. What did I

mean to ask? *Ask anything*, she offered. I'll try

now: of what apologies and places are we made, what terrifying Americas

haven't I heard of. Why? Because

we need a different listening? I hear right now

decades later the song a man nearby was singing to his baby girl, low

enough I could not make words out then and so slow

I struggled to hear a landing, just one soft rhyme.

I wanted to ask your brother's mother for an ending, but our time

was up. How calmly that man sang, as if time were

free or adequate, as if notes, hope, somewhere some answer—

STAMPEDE

Dirty Q-tip bobs in the pool, surprise—
    confusion of cotton, someone else's waxy sunrise—

        greetings, swimmers! Here, bitter throats, smog
            hovers over and even under water. Youth? A cloudy bog

        of remembered, slogged through, now this pace
       comes as an amber shock, age, sudden gun cocked icy vice closing a race

    chalk finish line. Swim harder. Metaphors: bleach
mixed with ammonia, blinding. Keep out of reach,

keep those kept out out in in wear this gas mask just in case
    water keeps filling up the space

        created by the paddles our hands make. Resistance
          is impossible, but still, resist. Language? A chance

         to come back, to become, nian
         stays *sticky* even if again

        what it means gets lost in my mind, forgotten, then
      what, crush of humans flutters straight toward when

    our glittering cities topple, when we trample flat a bunch of
bodies on the dock, in this case eighty. New Year's at the port. Hey, look above

the surface of the water. Floating objects make a light show, shadow
            object, shadow, body, guesswork. Circle back to man, to made, know

            we are this giant line of bodies falling
                    —calling names in every language, calling—

DRIVING LESSON, 1984

My father stood behind him
on the tractor, slim
and bearded, calm when

Jake accelerated upon hearing
the word *brake*. Flipping
the tractor wasn't the worst thing

that would ever happen to either
of them. In fact, they would recover
in an instant, jump off, neither

pinned under until later
when Jacob said, *It's cancer*
on the phone with our father.

Then, Jake was 23. That's how the weight
of a tractor can black a dad's light,
flip him over, blow his engine out.

DIALYSIS

The night Des tore her hair out, it was literal.
White sheets beneath her lit the hospital,

black strands deadly on that disinfected landscape.
Tubes rose from her chest, a band of cloth tape

over the port in her heart. Her body in bed
looked tiny—all her blood went out, came in. She said,

The women in my family are all cursed. Cyprus:
her grandma walked into a lake, carving traces

on the water's ugly surface. When she drowned, her
village was sorry for talk about a lover

she'd never had. Her mother's curse? To call. I pick
the phone up. She is far away, can't help, is sick

herself, so I slip out to say Des is asleep, OK,
then hang up dizzy with my lie and Des's *Get away*

*from me, the fuck away from me, please get me out
of here!* She's screaming, ripping at her hair. I shout

for a nurse who runs and plunges into the box of blood
something that makes Des still. The nurse says, *Good,*

but I'm wracked because we hate being quieted. Lights
sweep the ceiling, pass by, cars like mine driving other nights.
Des and I are both twenty-five.
Only I don't know that she'll die.

REPORT CARDS OF THE NOT QUITE DEAD

B+ patterns suggest my aliveness lately,
      the letters of license plates spell out for me
           genes no one else has or feels or can see.

Lazy Susans spin dying routines of our days:
      wash your hair, eat, teach, scan the familiar buffets
           of what becomes nothing we sing all the ways

in which small gathers big gathers beauty, try this:
      symmetrical butterfly wings in a kiss,
           the last breath of a letter, slight wisp of a wish,

slide and calcify into the habits, take each
      folded shirt, swallowed bite, Monday white, reeking bleach,
           Tuesday's blue as a vast twist of Michigan beach.

Wait for Wednesday, blurred yellow, about to arrive,
      swarming light around women—days sting us alive,
           senses crossing will offer up ways to contrive

enough projects and children and words to survive.

In a shadow in elementary school,
      we played jacks in a circle, scraped metal as cruel
           as our hands, open mouths, ritual chanted rule:

Ticktock, the game is locked, nobody else can play.
      And if they do, I'll take my shoe
           and knock them black and blue.

49

My eyes are white mothballs now, hard rolling orbs,
        some cells have turned turncoat, this body absorbs
                its own skin, hides its lesions, six biopsies, cores

that reveal exactly what margins to clear.
        The dark plays a film in which I disappear
                just as each of us has to, but when and to where?

Maybe head both directions: before now, after when.
        Make a baby who carries my face, and what then?
                I was dead to begin with; what's being dead again?

Doctors say that removal is not the hard part.
        Amputation's external; rebuilding's the art.

WITHOUT

Teach me to love without irony or violence,
and I'll sing you
   a city with waves on the drive
     like icy chimes, listen—
        how many notes shatter as they reach the shore. Cold
        enough water actually stacks. Get in
   with me, freeze, suffer, thaw. Let me love you without
     believing as I used to that we're safe, may last. Instead,
     let's peel, strip raw, find what matters, move against
     each other and whatever this is. If I could dissolve
       the words I use to hide, I would
write you hovering above me, tubes moving fluid from wounds I could not see
     without the lights in my mind
        shorting—they short here too, go black, and yet
      you looked, took those drains on, stripped them, tackled
   the project of my body by way of language, measured, counted
      milligram chances, wishing to statistic us
         straight back to the other oblivion, you
         stayed you after magicians sawed me open, sewed me
         back together, you kept all that we agreed
    on when we—stunningly young—said no matter what. Who knows what
     what becomes, how vast cold hot impossible, how much
     of our own blood. In plastic bulbs, or moving through
       us, submerged, blue. Teach me to love the way you do,
    white tape, clean gauze, let me see endless,
    see so many hazy days now clearing, now the lake is ice
    again, now winter. Frozen waves are chipping at each other,

sharp and gray. But high up we are dancing, reassembled,
brave because surprise
keeps us—our minds and marrow lit—alive.

HORSE FAIR

Sky turned circus, dim five. Night
rides opened, horses draped
with ribbons lined up, eyes flashing
moonlight. They were in a contest
our silly pony always lost.
Freedom made us grave, yet let us ride
the Ferris wheel, neon veins alit,
sit high atop shellacked pink backs of ponies
on a carousel. The one I always chose posed
in a scream, victorious head
thrown back with force enough to bare
square, painted teeth. My hands around his neck, I rode
in circles until spots formed in my vision and we landed
on fact: a plastic horse outlasts us.
We wilt; he shines.
We left the grounds
each year at midnight, sticky shreds
of cotton candy on us and behold—the marks of our small fingers
everywhere. Safely elsewhere, present now I wonder
which of those ponies did stay put. In pitch night,
maybe mine raged away,
tore off his pole still twisting up and up,
no longer through his stomach out his back, no fear.
Imagine: no fear!
Now I've made it so it happened. Here.

YOU WROTE YOUR OWN OBITUARY

A final chance to tell the truth, for once, and yet
then what? You want *vibrant, immortal, real*, must set

      records of yourself not straight but layered,
      floating, far from all that he/she/they heard

from logistics, from receipts as pdfs so
no one else doctors them. The doctors know

      you're doomed; they knew. How many hours barking
      into phones: insurance, taxes, teeth, skin, parking,

truth might be bureaucracy. Oh god, you want to
write you lived/blazed/loved/sexed highways right through

      early decades, gobbled like a monstrous, hungry
      bird at everything delicious, were so angry

fury torched your marrow. *Political, emotional,*
and sometimes *justifiable*. Write it: *memorable?*

      Trouble wasn't daily, please god never believed
      in, wasn't sixty million dishes washed, bags heaved

in bins, shampoo swirls, leaves raked, crab apples at
your parents' house, parades of desks and chairs you sat

      in, not opposition to yourself but once's. Seven
      hours once you stared out the train window, even

though fat stack on your lap of papers yet to grade,
phone throbbing with the endless calls you should have made,

      once you were a body of water weeping for the boy
      with floppy hair, once junior high, once every night was every small toy

you stacked and gathered for your babies. Once the days
were milk and rocking, sleepy sleepless ways

      to find some sleep, to clock. Once? Now count how
      many peacocks in a biblical garden, now

they jump from trees in your imagination, you
remember them even though dead, the blue

      and gold one screaming from the branches, full plummet—
      white one underneath a terrible blur of movement.

How they fanned themselves, delighted and wild
as you once were, once old, once child,

      once sun came down like liquid on you and
      your baby, shaping mermaids out of sand:

shell bra cups, seaweed hair, black rocks for
eyes. Your own eyes reading, seeking, seeing more

      of something you can't quite remember, can't return
      to, get back or keep track of, bits of light, nocturne

maybe, but this flash will remain, not yours to say
what was or wants to burn, what wants to stay.

DEAR GERYON

Oh small red monster, wings and pictures, Rabbit

Giggle tied with ribbon,

fly you shot for fifteen minutes,

keeping alive what dies and dies: you're

real. Subject, not just object, not just monster, not just

letters, high above this/that life, you are what

I am a stick figure, big eyed, lost suddenness of twenties, a grown-up not grown up,

here and alone, my words/days, numbers/colors, danger. I am

adjectival license, always in my own mind

choosing words. I wear a giant

helmet most days. I am on your island, terrified

of Herakles because he kills you and your little dog for no reason

(except assigned to, just one of his labors). Who wants a guy

who does what he is told? Not you. Not me. I don't want

you to die. I will glitter with your wishes, senses, lost word *each*, plump sculpture, your tomato smoking, Mama, your Mama sometimes

feels like me or mine. Geryon, seems to me that changing our minds this

many times is the opposite of dying.

My Mondays, always white, and Tuesday's blue,

take new hues only when I'm with you. News:

you show the world on an axis not the one we knew.

Now roses shriek in sunlight, I shriek, mornings

pour the world back and forth, our loneliness gets contradicted, lava bubbles over.

Please fuse new atoms, fragile monster, keep making meaning,

looking out, up, down, around, a million photons moving keep you

keep your wings and life my own

bright guides for ways to change, to make

what matters most, be brave.

DEAR ALICE

I'm writing from the milk life,

    new life, gauzy frontier after that other life

        is never coming back. Come back, old life.

            Wait, don't. I need what I've made, cannot reverse, see

                everything awaits me. Can you help, maybe?

My mind is in my body, Alice, nouns:

        stacked plastic trucks, biblical chickens clucking, all these neighbors,

           girlfriends, books, a crowd or two of women, virgins, whores

              some of them me, my daughters, planets, scores

of gossiping mouths. I heard Gertrude was a gossip, sometimes mean, heard

    she got words drunk and let them

        do what crazy shit they maybe meant to anyway. To that I say,

           uninhibited is hot, but you're the one I want. The one

           behind the one. I'm behind one too, I'm your cool secret

           in shadow. Even lives I choose

enrage me. Alice? Were you

furious? Wife, wife. Did you hide

so she could shine and shatter

language but not say

that she was Jewish, not say not

French, not say anything that might have

hurt her? What hurt you? What I don't know

hurts most, turns out. That's my problem.

Another? I am granular, a single grain, a stroke mark, radical,

one flutter of somebody else's pulse bouncing around my cage of bones.

Move closer to me, please, I can't hear you,

I'm writing *time*, I'm writing *trying*—thick, choke, alone, blood blue,

I'll recognize your voice when it comes through.

PARTING AT CHANGGAN

Translated from Li Bai's 长干行

My hair still in bangs, I played outside the front gate,
picking flowers. You came by, high on a bamboo hobbyhorse,
then sat playing with our green plums. We lived like this
together in Changgan, two little ones, no jealousy, no distrust.

At fourteen, I married you. So shy my face
never opened up, I just lowered my head
and watched the dark wall. You called to me
a thousand times, but I never answered your call.

At fifteen, I answered, looked up, unfurrowed, wanted
to mingle together, even past our mortal days, wanted
forever, knew we would cling faithfully to our moorings.
So why climb the watchtower looking for you?

But at sixteen, you left. You went far away, to Yanyudui,
where churning waters crash the rocky shores.
For five months now, no you. All of nature echoes
the gibbons, crying out in sorrow.

Outside our gate your footprints fill with moss, each step too deep to be
erased. Too early, leaves fall in rough autumn wind. It's only
August, yet the butterflies lose color. Still, they fly
in pairs to the Western Garden, as I pale too, aging. They hurt me

so much, sitting here. If you are on your way, please
send word when. If you have passed the fast currents
of the Yangtze, I will think nothing of the distance—
I'll come all the way to Changfengsha to meet you again.

POWER OF THE POWERLESS

Translated from Cui Jian's 无能的力量

Soon as you say *do*—you do.
Leave faster
than an angel flies, to
and fro. Your horizon's wide—
mine's narrow, see?
I can't even tell if you're into me.

I do it all, but nothing's done.
I'm not relaxed or free.
I still daydream I'll change an era—
but I'm still powerless,
and you're waiting.
If I fail, will you still want me?

You watch me silently.
Say nothing, wordlessly
drop your hand to catch my hand
and hold it soft and tight.
Then you make it a fist,
raise it to your lips
and bite.

I only brag, still cannot lie.
The sky's pitch black—
the light's too bright.
I've already lost my way.
Please keep close by,
make me look OK.

The wind begins to blow faint hope.
I'm like the wind. You're waves.
Rolling water beneath my caress,
can you feel this power, so powerless?

You watch me silently,
say nothing, wordlessly
drop your hand to catch my hand
and hold it soft and tight.
Then you make it a fist,
raise it to your lips
and bite.

FROM YOUR MAMA AT FIRST

Here the sweet sweep and scope of one body
becomes another, bright change underway
already. Say you'll be my baby, say
elbow, kneecap, eyes, and spine. Come and play

a game of antique, stunning love. Your ways
will be new rules, our own sudden always
imaginable only once this daze
takes over, only after your pace, craze

the milk life, words unmoored, contradiction
everywhere. Light, power, which prediction
could have guessed your slipping lisping diction,
your fantastic tempers, predilection

list: penguins, kissing, each bubble popping,
such stock you teach me to take—unstopping—

NEXT UP

Daisy chain of childhood days, the cadence
of rain, spring, hours of our rocking dance—
I still move side to side all these years since
on train platforms, at street lights, every chance

a memory of carrying you. Window
on 113th, the fire trucks below:
tiny men running like toys, each hero
you liked to name, each dog too, baby, row

of flowers, biblical, St. John's. Fountain
of mythical creatures, carved stone mountain,
sun atop it. Real peacocks. Once when
you were four, the white one leaped, screamed again

and again from a tree. You said, *Maybe*
it lost its mother. A warning to me.

IMAGINING

for Emily and Ronan

To all who say *I can't imagine what*
you must be feeling, to those who ask that
question: *How'd you survive?*, say *brave*, say *but*
I'd never be able to manage what

you have, I say no. Climb up with me now,
saddle up this grief, imagine. Here's how
we stay human even torched by sorrow:
stare at my (it might be your) tomorrow,

ride back to the whisper of his baby
laugh, two milk teeth, silky feet, life maybe
contained in what we call gone, but give me
this: feel of his belly, slippery,

swimming in my arms, give me each sweet note
of his breathing—imagine us—afloat—

ONCE CONSCIOUS

Filament, corridor, some gossamer
dots will still connect us even once we're
not together, even once—I know per
early storms of your wisdom that you're sure

of who you are, I am, so many hours
we dissolved mine, yours, until all was ours,
then you wobbled and toddled off. Powers
beyond my range. Your own feet, legs, towers

of self! You gathered words as I had, at
three I said, *housework is boring*, and that
you (my mom) *love it, so you're boring*, sat
in the way of her mop, mean logic, flat

out: now you're sharp, sweetly conscious of
how we're no longer one—in spite of love.

MY MOTHER COMES BACK TO ME

At the kitchen table of my childhood
she spends her only quiet moments, food
prepared, my brothers still asleep. I would
like closed-captioned text, her mind if I could

read, please. Her thumb pressed against her lip,
my firecracker of a mother, slip
skinny, racing through days of teaching, whip-
quick rocket always lit as if the tip

of her is a wick, ready for impact,
her very being ignited by a pact
with us. I used to be her. Embrace fact:
I'm becoming her again, the world cracked

open by time, strange light, daughters aligned—
a constellation, our silt selves refined.

TOO

Sing a song of sense, this surface

      of the lake, roiling water, lolling cusp

            of summer, maybe dawning wonder we are late

to join. Chorus of us. Women

      spackled, rageful, wracked, we sparkle,

            undercurrents of unutterable

language coming up. Come up. From buried, sunk, from fear,

      link words, make stable something, here:

            when we don't, when we do, when this,

when shut up, when beat wordless, when

      we're silent with what's senseless, bound toward dirt, erased,

            diminished. When we erase to sleep, swim, cope,

when we learn how to choke

      down rage, pain, want, when not allowed to name,

            when eating (is a) failure, when we breathe or speak,

when daring, flawed, disgusting or averting too,

when, too, then flee it, *flee*. Come with us. Ride

this grief, ride pride to some reach safe

from eating our own, from hunting what we never

meant to be. Mean it. Don't pack words

in your furious marrow, shout out

what we made: language, all the babies, hell, ourselves.